# 125 Christmas O Patterns

## for the Scroll Saw

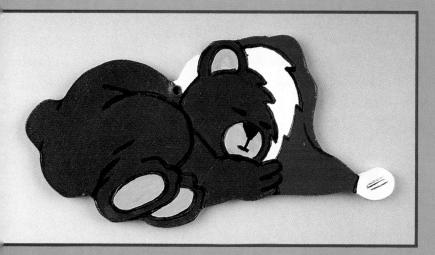

Arthur L. Grover

*Schiffer Publishing Ltd*

880 Lower Valley Rd. Atglen, PA 19310 USA

*Designed by Bonnie M. Hensley*

ISBN: 0-7643-0323-6
Printed in China

## Contents

Published by Schiffer Publishing Ltd.
4880 Lower Valley Road
Atglen, PA 19310
Phone: (610) 593-1777; Fax: (610) 593-2002
E-mail: schifferbk@aol.com
Please write for a free catalog.
This book may be purchased from the publisher.
Please include $3.95 for shipping.
Try your bookstore first.

We are interested in hearing from authors
with book ideas on related subjects.

# WELCOME TO 125 CHRISTMAS ORNAMENT PATTERNS FOR THE SCROLL SAW

Using this book, you will be able to make any of these ornaments you wish using a limited amount of woodworking tools and equipment. The sizes of the ornaments have been varied, but you can make them in any size you wish. If you would like to group a few of the same size ornaments, cut the patterns out of the book and scotch tape them together then have them enlarged or reduced for you to work with.

As you look over this book, you should remember you are not going to try to become an artist by painting these designs. Instead, I like to refer to it as learning to *paint by area*. This means that the lines on all of these ornaments should be kept dark so you can see the different areas to paint. When you start painting, be sure to re-draw any lines that you cover up. Each ornament should be given two coats as you paint in the design. Between each coat of paint, redefine each line so you can see them on the second coat. I use a little heavier line of black for the final lines, as this helps to make the ornament stand out more on the Christmas tree. Again, you can do what you like and make them your own "personal ornament."

You do not have to follow the painting scheme I show on my ornaments. If you like one in particular, make multiple copies and paint them different colors; change the eyes from back dots to regular eyes, etc.

In some cases, you will see that I antiqued the Santas. This is done after you have finished painting and putting the polyurethane on them. After the poly has dried for at least twenty-four hours, I take a large paint brush and some walnut or mahogany water based stain (shaken and stirred up good) and dip the brush into it. I then blot on a paper towel to get any of the access off, then lightly drag it over the face of the ornament and leave just a light coat on.

I am a commercial artist by day and a professional musician on weekends (for over thirty years). I became tired of all the traveling with bands, but when I stopped my musical career I needed something to occupy my free time so I began to design needlepoint kits (which were sold worldwide) and then I started my woodworking career thanks to my father's influence.

In 1988 I published an article in *Doll Reader* (an international magazine) on my Santa ornaments that were holding dolls. The response to that article requested more designs from a lot of the readers and they suggested I put together a book on them. I started to, but I didn't have the time to do it then. However, I began to sketch ideas from time to time and put them away for future use.

In 1996 I started to assemble all my designs of the ornaments and I made roughly 500 of them which I gave to friends and relatives. I used them as name tags for presents (that's where I painted the back side white with a flat interior latex paint that I could write on (**do not coat the back with polyurethane**) and the rest I put on my tree. After Christmas, I started to do pen and ink patterns trying to keep the designs to a minimum amount of sharp points with as little fancy scroll work as possible. I think the designs in the book show that was accomplished.

Remember, I designed these patterns for anyone to be able to do. If you make a cut a little too deep here or there, when you paint the ornaments most of these faults will not show up, so before you discard any of them, be sure it was beyond the point of saving. I can only remember one or two ornaments I couldn't save over all the years. A few years back, our family Christmas tree was decorated with better than 50% of the ornaments I had designed and made. Everyone who saw the tree remarked on how unique it was.

# WHAT YOU WILL NEED

**Supplies necessary to make ornaments:**

Wood - either 1/8" (3.2mm) masonite or 1/4" (6.4mm)
Luan Plywood
Latex White Paint (any type - Indoor/exterior)
Graphite Tracing Paper
Pencils - #4 Hard Lead and #2 Soft Lead
Small and Medium Point Artist Paint Brushes
Masking Tape
Polyurethane Water Based - Matte or Glossy
Acrylic or Latex Paints (These can be purchased at a
    local craft store in small bottles for less than
    $1.50-$2.00 a bottle. You can make shades by
    adding white or black to paints.)
        Red
        Yellow
        Blue
        White
        Flesh
        Black
        Gold
        Brown
        Green
        Silver

**Equipment needed for ornaments:**

Scroll Saw (If you don't have one maybe you can find
    someone who does and have them cut out the de
    signs for you.)
Fine Sandpaper
Electric Drill
1/8" (3.2mm) Drill Bit with brad point (for making holes
    to hang ornaments - *be sure to drill slow for a nice
    clean hole!*)

**Optional Items:**

Elmer's or craft glue that dries clear
Different color Glitter (tubes can be found at craft stores
Gold or Silver heavyweight cord for making hangers
Green, Red *or any* colored Felt

*Note: If you only plan on painting one side of the
ornament, you should have green paint to paint the
reverse side!*

# PREPARATION

I bought a 4 foot (609.6 mm) by 8 foot (2438.4 mm) piece of 1/8" (3.2 mm) piece of masonite (hardboard) at the lumberyard and had them cut the sheet to 2 feet (609.6 mm) by 4 feet (609.6 mm) pieces. I then brought the wood home and painted the boards. For the designs I was going to paint on **both sides**, I painted the piece with two coats of white on both sides. On the ornaments I was only going to paint on **one side** I painted the front side with two coats of white and the back side with two coats of green paint.

While the board(s) were drying, I cut the designs out of the book leaving anywhere from 1/2" (12.7 mm) to 1" (25.4 mm) all the way around the design. This is so I could tape the designs to the board and have enough room to slide the tracing paper under them and still copy the design. After the board had dried I taped the design at the top on two sides leaving room to slide the tracing paper (face down) under the design. With a hard #4 pencil I traced the full design, then raising the design and graph paper (but not taking it off) I checked to be sure I had copied the full design. If not, I lowered the design and put the tracing paper back under it and traced the missing area. When it was complete, I then took the design and tape off and removed the design and graph paper. I then started the next design about 1" (25.4 mm) away from the other design and repeated the steps until I had filled the rest of the board.

When you have traced all the designs and filled the board (you can make duplicates or as many copies of each design as you want to make), take a soft #2 pencil and trace all the designs on the board to define them better. This will make it easier to cut them out and easier to start painting.

When you have cut them out the patterns (or found someone to cut them out for you), take the fine sandpaper and sand the edges smooth. For masonite you have to use a sharp 1/8" (3.2 mm) drill bit to drill holes in the top of each design for the hangers. Go Slow! - you need a nice smooth hole!

## BACKSIDE INFORMATION

If you are going to paint the backside of the ornaments, cut the actual outline of the ornament and tape the design to the back side of the ornament wrapping the tape over the sides so you can trace it again. Be sure to use to the soft lead #2 pencil and make the lines heavy so they can be seen.

If you want your design to be two-sided, copy the same design on the backside by putting the graph paper under the design face up, and copy it. Tape that to the ornament and use the backside just as you traced your original design.

## PAINTING INFORMATION

You have the option of painting the ornaments *any color* you wish. You can follow the design colors shown here or use your own choices in painting the ornaments. You can mix colors (such as red and white to obtain pink, white and black to obtain gray, etc.) or buy additional colors at the craft store. I tried to vary the colors on my ornaments; on some Santa suits I painted pure red, while on others I added a little black to make it a darker red, and I did the same with other styles such as the snowmen. On some of these I painted the hats black, others I painted brown, some I gave round dots for eyes, others I gave half circles, etc. Be sure to keep redefining the black separation lines between colors. In most cases, you should give each color two coats before adding the details, such as eyes, etc. When you have finished, follow the lines with a wide stroke brush in black paint to make the lines heavy so they will show up on the Christmas tree.

I used plastic lids off coffee cans, sour cream, butter containers, etc. for mixing my paints. When it got messy I threw them away and used new ones. For cleaning my brushes I used empty coffee cans, plastic butter containers, sour cream bottoms, etc.

When I started to paint the ornaments, I usually started with white as my first color. I painted every area on each ornament that I wanted white (I usually did ten to fifteen ornaments at a time), making sure I painted the edges the same color. By the time I had finished with the last one I could go back to the first one that was dry and paint the next lightest color and repeat the process. The last color I painted was always the darkest, usually black. I then redefined the lines, and either gave the ornaments a second coat the same way, being sure my paint brush was very clean before starting with white. When the second coats were dry I then painted the lines with black and added the details. If I painted the back side, I then turned them over after they had dried and painted them the same way.

When the front side (or both sides) were dry, I usually waited 24 hours and then gave the ornaments, including the edges, a coat of polyurethane to protect it. Again, I gave it two coats. If I had painted the back side in colors I also gave it two coats of polyurethane, being careful not to allow runs on the sides or on front.

## OPTIONS FOR NOT PAINTING BACKSIDE

You have two options for the backside if you aren't going to paint the design on the back:

1. Paint the backside with green paint. If you painted the back side green initially, then check it and see if it needs to be touched up. It usually does from sanding the edge. The green will blend in with the tree if the ornament happens to turn on the tree. (I usually bend the metal hanger to prevent this from happening.)

2. The second option is to take the ornament and trace the edge on a piece of felt. (Red, green or any color will do.) Cut the outline out and pin it to the piece of felt. Take the pinking shears and cut approximately 1" (25.4 mm) around the outline (try to line up the back teeth of the pinking shears with the cut so you have a uniform edge all around the ornament). Place the felt on newspaper, add the glue to the backside of the ornament, center the ornament over the piece of felt and press it with the glue side down on the felt. Put a book or some sort of weight on it to hold it until it dries.

**SPECIAL NOTE:** When I made my first ornaments in 1988, we had a new fireplace added to our house and I had a lot of 3/8" (9.5 mm) pieces of siding that was 10" (254 mm) wide plywood. I used the siding and cut out my first ornaments and painted them. My ornaments were then already twenty-five years old and antique! I used a lot of different scraps of wood around the house and found they made unique ornaments to hang on the front door, in the picture window, etc.

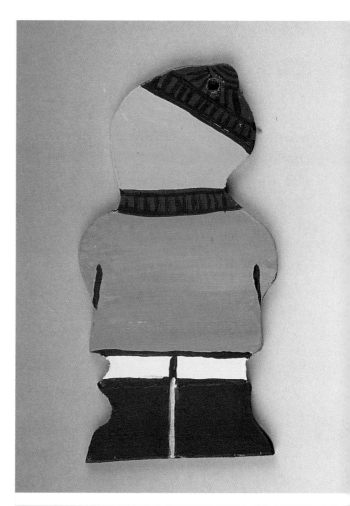

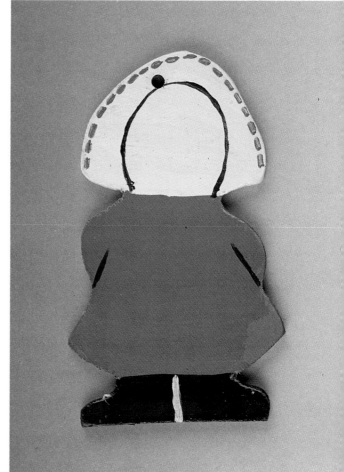

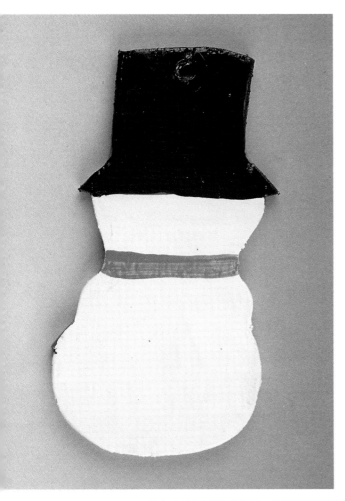

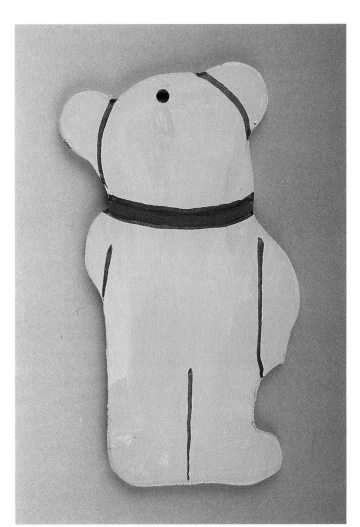

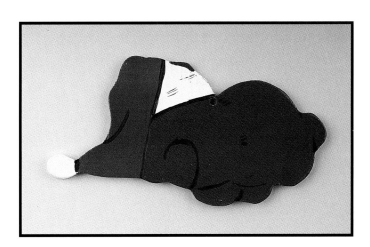

11

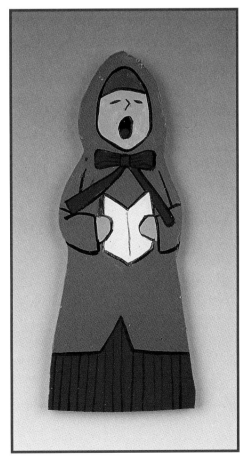

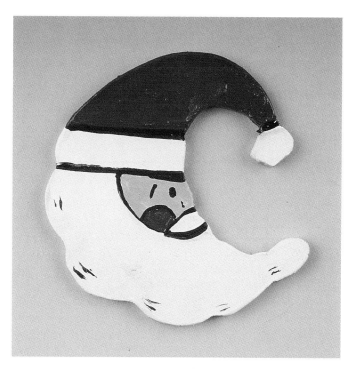

14

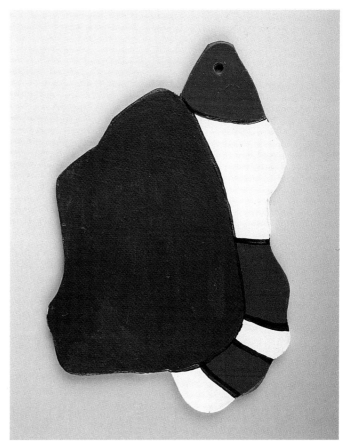

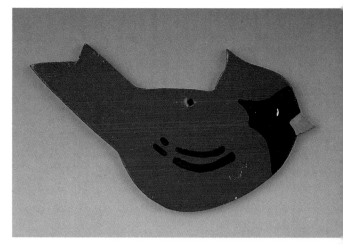

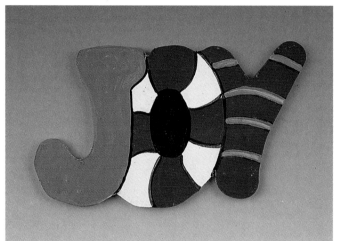
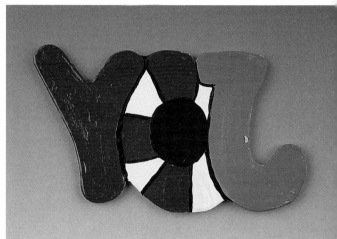

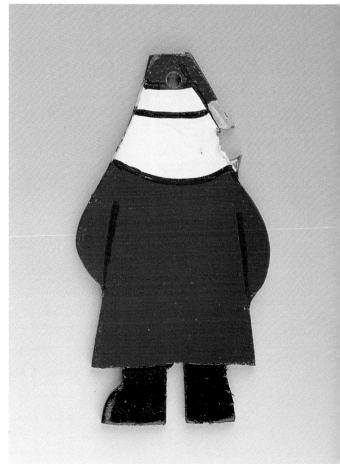

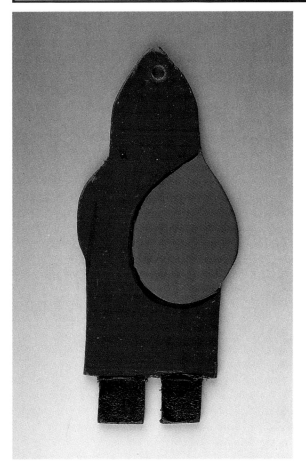

17

 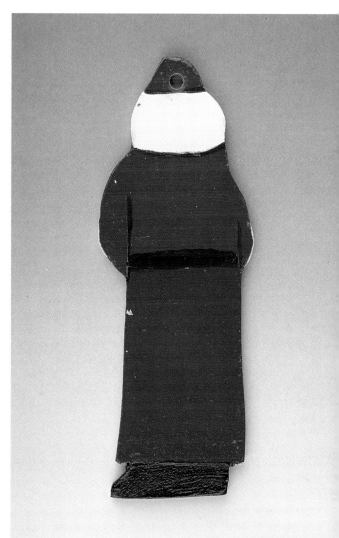

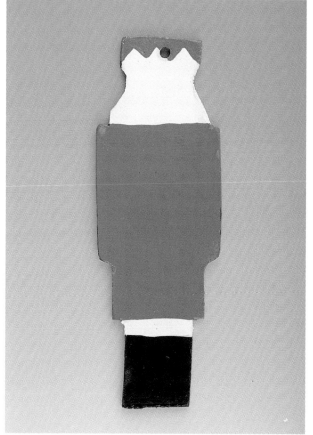

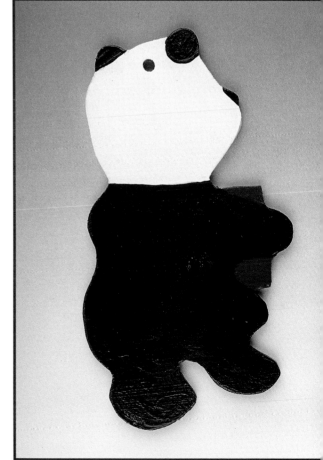

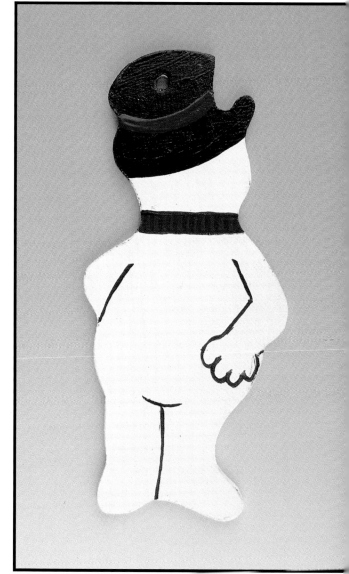

# Painted Patterns

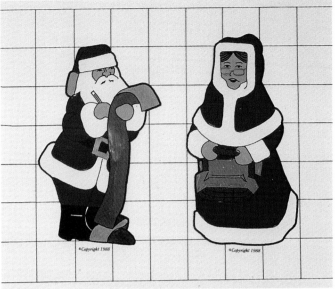

28

© Copyright 1988

© Copyright 1988

© Copyright 1988

© Copyright 1988

© Copyright 1988 by Grovers' Studio

© Copyright 1988 by Grovers' Studio

© Copyright 1988 by Grovers' Studio

© Copyright 1988 by Grovers' Studio

© Copyright 1988 by Grovers' Studio

© Copyright 1988 by Grovers' Studio

# Black and White Patterns

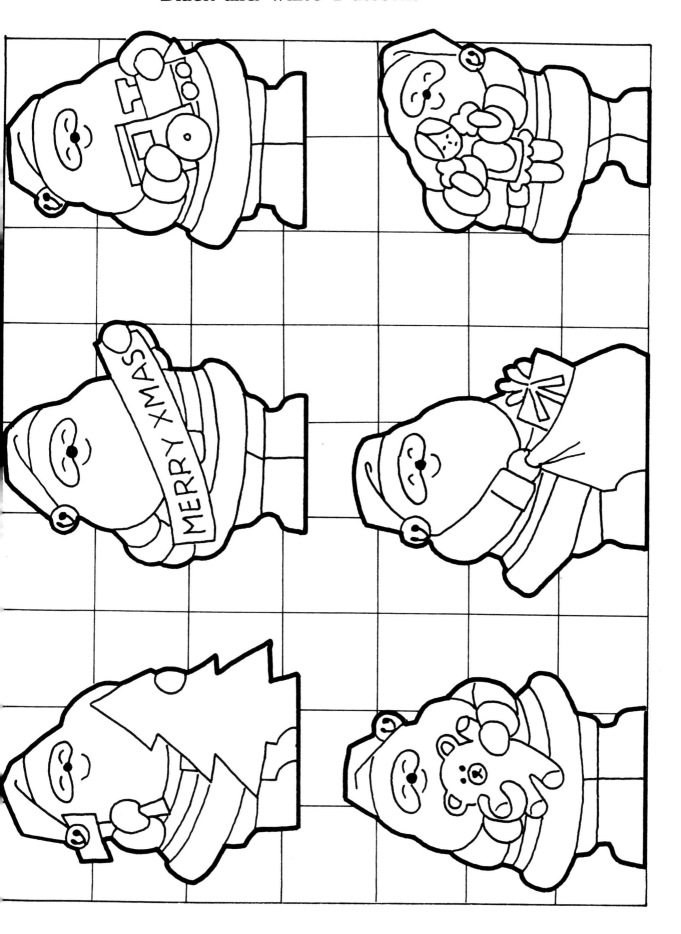

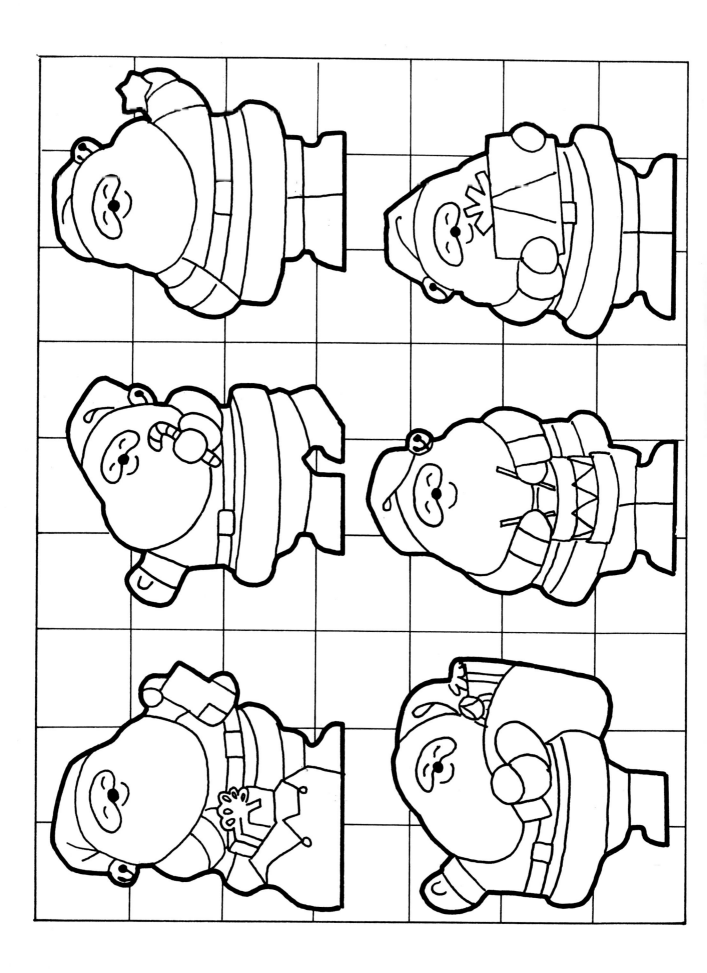

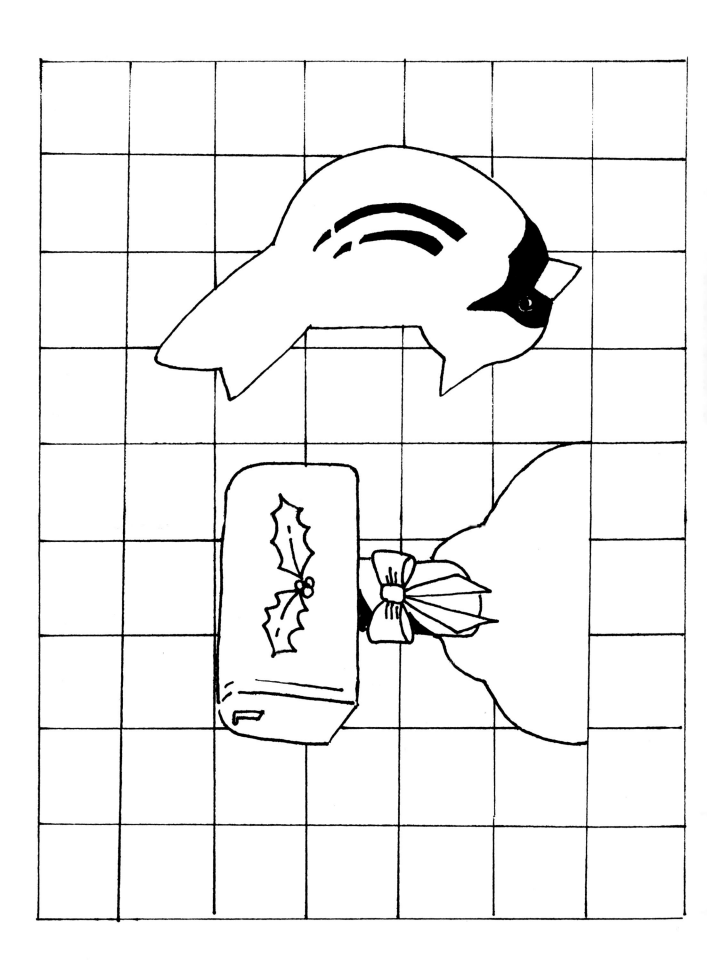

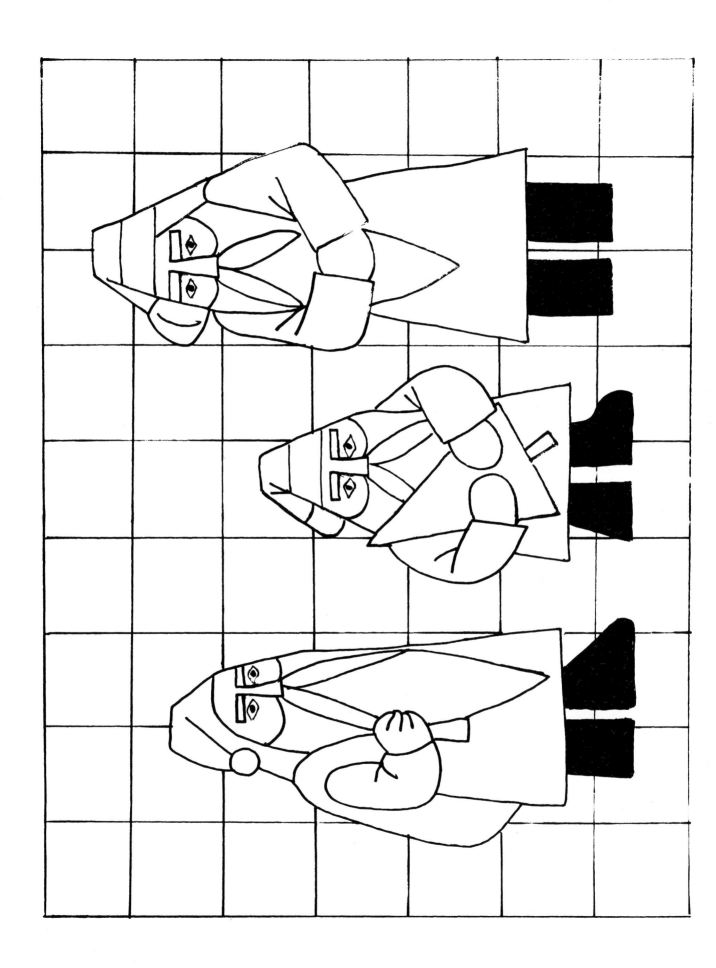

48

51

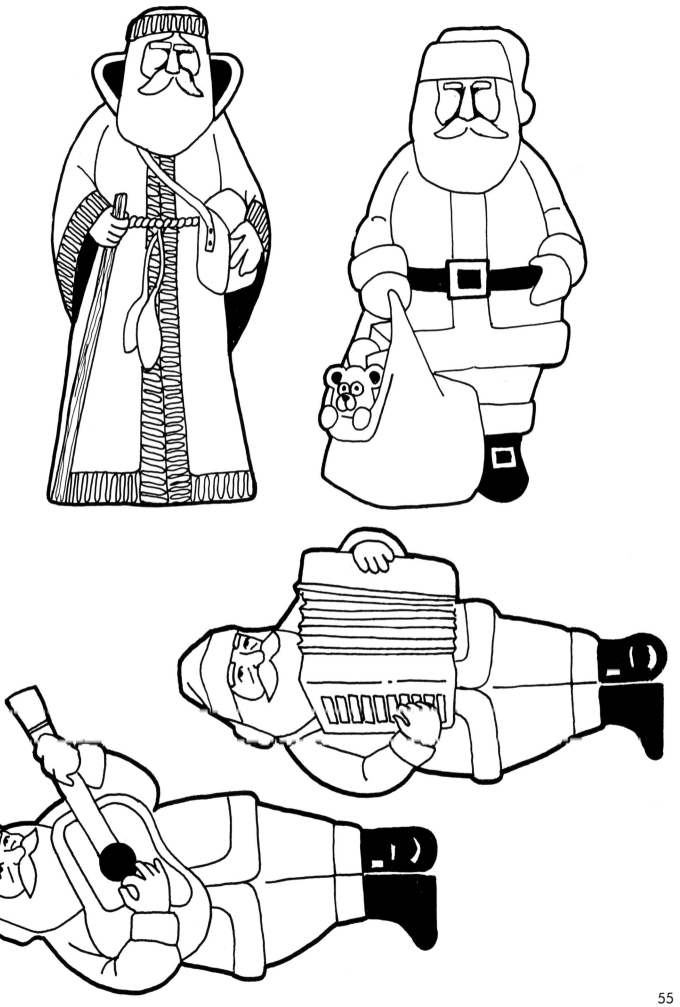

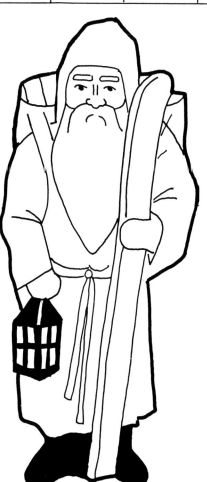